Phonetic F

The Chris

Luk

M000013858

Jesus Is Born!

Claudia Courtney ☆ **Illustrated by Chris Sharp**

CPH

SAINT LOUIS

Note to Grown-ups

The love of reading is one of the greatest things you can instill in your child. It opens new horizons, exposes your child to new ideas, and provides information as well as entertainment.

This beginning reader series blends the best of two worlds—phonics to help your child learn to read and popular Bible stories to help your child learn to read God's Word. After you use a book in this series, open your child's Bible and read the story from God's Word. Emphasize to your child that this story is not make-believe—it's true, and we can believe every word in God's Holy Book.

Before you begin, review together the word, sound, and spelling lists on page 16. This story emphasizes the phoneme that makes the short ŭ sound as in run.

After your review, read the story to your child, exaggerating the designated phonetic sound or sounds. Discuss the illustrations. Your enthusiasm for reading, and especially for reading God's Word, should be contagious. Run your finger under each word as you read it, showing your child that it is the words that convey the actual story. Have your child join with you in reading repeated phrases.

Finally, have your child read the story as you offer plenty of praise. Pause to allow your youngster time to sound out words, but provide help when necessary to avoid frustration. When a mistake is made, invite your child to reread the sentence. This provides an appropriate opportunity to guide your early reader.

Please remember that your child is learning and blending a complex set of new skills. Early success and your generous praise are keys to opening the door to your child's world of reading, especially to the joys of reading the Bible.

Claudia Courtney

The shepherds hummed and strummed to their fluffy sheep. Time for supper. Time for slumber.

4

Sell your books at sellbackyourBook.com!

Go to sellbackyourBook.com and get an instant price quote. We even pay the shipping - see what your old books are worth today!

Inspected By:moni

00019683756

0001968 **3756**

G

Hush! Hush! Hush!

Suddenly, shepherds bumped
and jumped.
Look up! Look up!

6

Hundreds of angels
filled the sky.
"Jesus is born!" they
trumpeted.

7

Shepherds rushed
to see Jesus.
Rush! Rush! Rush!

8

Run and run.
Huff and puff.

They found Jesus in a humble
    stable.
Animals munched and
    crunched.
They gulped and grunted.

10

Shepherds clustered
to see Jesus bundled
in a manger.

Mary hugged and cuddled Jesus.
She tucked in His blanket,
all snug.

Hush! Hush! Hush!

13

Shepherds worshiped Jesus.
We can worship Him too.
We can tell of Jesus.

Jesus is born!

phoneme *u*

bumped	hummed	snug
bundled	hundreds	strummed
clustered	hush	suddenly
crunched	Jesus	supper
cuddled	jumped	trumpeted
fluffy	munched	tucked
grunted	puff	up
gulped	run	
huff	rush	
hugged	rushed	
humble	slumber	

Other Words

a	His	stable
all	in	tell
and	is	the
angels	look	their
animals	manger	they
blanket	Mary	time
born	of	to
can	see	too
filled	she	we
for	sheep	worship
found	shepherds	worshiped
Him	sky	